EXPLORE THE FANTASTIC WORLD OF

UNDERWATER ANIMALS

PICTURE ENCYCLOPEDIA

Wonder House

GREAT WHITE SHARK

The Great White Shark is a powerful predator with a sleek, torpedo-shaped body, gray on top and white underneath. They can grow up to 20ft (6m) long and weigh up to 5,000lb (2,268kg)! These sharks have sharp, triangular teeth and a strong tail that helps them swim fast, up to 35mph (56kph). They mostly eat fish, Seals and Sea Lions. They live in coastal waters around the world. Their lifespan can vary from 30–70 years. Great Whites belong to the ***Lamnidae*** family and their scientific name is ***Carcharodon carcharias***.

BULL SHARK

Bull Shark is a large and powerful Shark known for its stocky body and broad, blunt snout. They typically grow around 7–11ft (2–3.3m) in length and weigh around 200–500lb (91–227kg). Bull sharks are highly adaptable, capable of living in both saltwater and freshwater environments. Their diet includes fish, Dolphins and even small Whales. Known for their speed, they can swim at speeds of up to 12mph (19kph). They are a member of the ***Carcharhinidae*** family with the scientific name ***Archarhinus leucas***.

DID YOU KNOW?

Bull Sharks get their name from their bull-like appearance and nature.

THRESHER SHARK

The Thresher Shark is known for its long, whip-like tail, which can be nearly as long as its body. These sleek predators can grow up to 20ft (6m) and can weigh 750lb (340kg) and above. Thresher Sharks are fast swimmers, reaching speeds of up to 60mph (96.5kph). They primarily feed on small fish and Squid, using their tails to stun prey. These sharks are found near the coasts and oceans, where they hunt in packs. They belong to the family ***Alopiidae*** and their scientific name is ***Alopias vulpinus***.

DID YOU KNOW?

The longest common thresher recorded was 25ft (7.6m).

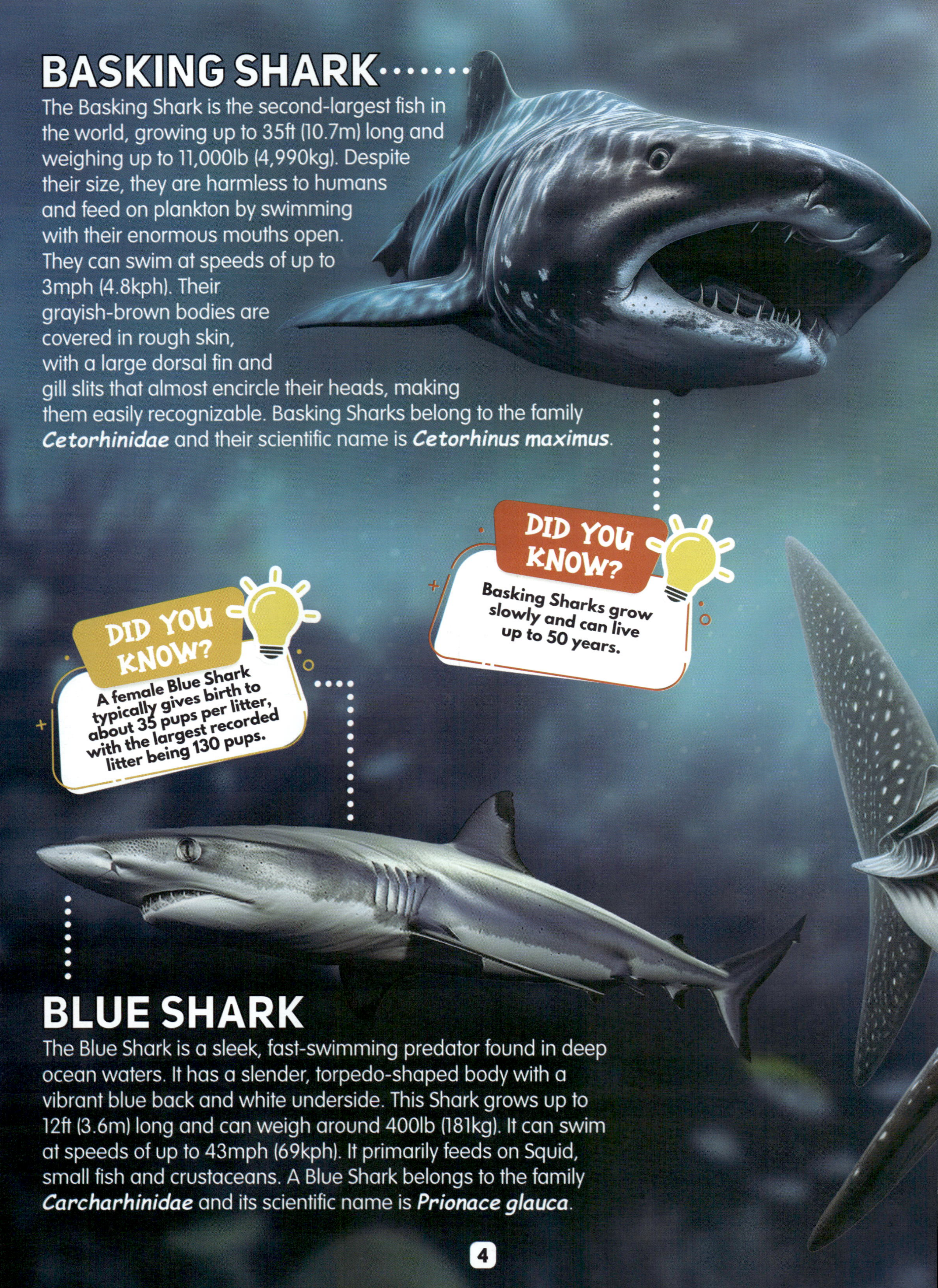

BASKING SHARK

The Basking Shark is the second-largest fish in the world, growing up to 35ft (10.7m) long and weighing up to 11,000lb (4,990kg). Despite their size, they are harmless to humans and feed on plankton by swimming with their enormous mouths open. They can swim at speeds of up to 3mph (4.8kph). Their grayish-brown bodies are covered in rough skin, with a large dorsal fin and gill slits that almost encircle their heads, making them easily recognizable. Basking Sharks belong to the family ***Cetorhinidae*** and their scientific name is ***Cetorhinus maximus***.

DID YOU KNOW?

Basking Sharks grow slowly and can live up to 50 years.

DID YOU KNOW?

A female Blue Shark typically gives birth to about 35 pups per litter, with the largest recorded litter being 130 pups.

BLUE SHARK

The Blue Shark is a sleek, fast-swimming predator found in deep ocean waters. It has a slender, torpedo-shaped body with a vibrant blue back and white underside. This Shark grows up to 12ft (3.6m) long and can weigh around 400lb (181kg). It can swim at speeds of up to 43mph (69kph). It primarily feeds on Squid, small fish and crustaceans. A Blue Shark belongs to the family ***Carcharhinidae*** and its scientific name is ***Prionace glauca***.

WHALE SHARK

The Whale Shark is the largest fish in the world, growing up to 40ft (12m) long and weighing around 20tn (18t).* Despite their size, they are gentle giants that feed on tiny plankton, small fish and Krill by filter-feeding through their wide mouths. Their bodies are covered in unique white spots and stripes over a bluish-gray skin. Whale Sharks can swim at speeds of about 3mph (4.8kph). Found in warm, tropical oceans, these Sharks can live for 70 years and more making them true ocean wanderers. They belong to the family ***Rhincodontidae*** and their scientific name is ***Rhincodon typus***.

DID YOU KNOW?

These sharks can gulp approximately 1,00,000gal (3,78,541L) of ocean water in a day.

* tn: tons
t: metric tons

TIGER SHARK

The Tiger Shark is a large, powerful predator found in tropical and subtropical oceans. It can grow up to 18ft (5.5m) long and weigh up to 1,400lb (635kg). Its body is streamlined with a distinct grayish-blue coloration and dark vertical stripes, giving it a tiger-like appearance. Known for its speed, it can swim up to 20mph (32kph). This Shark has a broad, blunt snout and serrated teeth designed to crush bones and shells. It is an opportunistic feeder, consuming fish, Sea Turtles, seabirds and even inedible items like tires. A Tiger Shark belongs to the family ***Carcharhinidae***. Its scientific name is ***Galeocerdo cuvier***.

DID YOU KNOW?

Tiger Sharks are merciless human attackers; second to the White Sharks.

HAMMERHEAD SHARK

The Hammerhead Shark is known for its unique, flattened, hammer-shaped head called a cephalofoil, which improves its vision and hunting abilities. They typically grow to about 13–20ft (4–6m) long and can weigh up to 1,000lb (454kg). There are 10 species of hammerhead sharks, ranging from small Bonnetheads to Great Hammerheads. The largest of the Hammerhead Shark species, the Great Hammerhead can swim at a speed of 25mph (40kph). They primarily feed on fish, Squid, Octopuses and Stingrays. Hammerheads belong to the family ***Sphyrnidae*** and the scientific name of the Great Hammerhead is ***Sphyrna mokarran***.

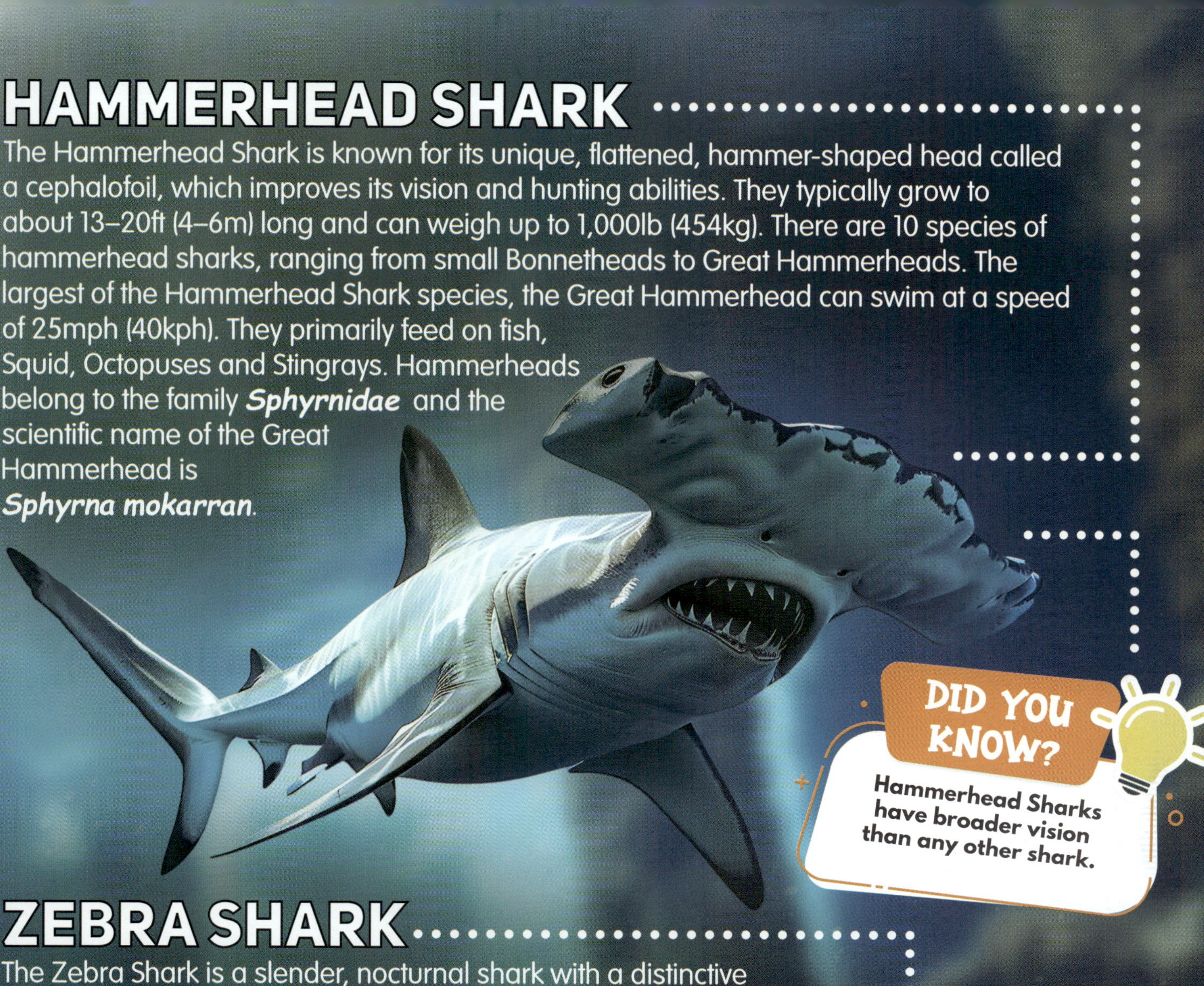

DID YOU KNOW?

Hammerhead Sharks have broader vision than any other shark.

ZEBRA SHARK

The Zebra Shark is a slender, nocturnal shark with a distinctive yellowish-brown body covered in dark spots as adults, while juveniles display zebra-like stripes. Zebra Sharks grow up to 8ft (2.4m) and weigh around 45lb (20kg). They are slow swimmers, reaching speeds of about 5mph (8kph). Their diet includes small fish, crustaceans and mollusks, which they hunt along coral reefs and sandy seafloors. They belong to the ***Stegostomatidae*** family and their scientific name is ***Stegostoma fasciatum***.

DID YOU KNOW?

Zebra Sharks are flexible and hide in between tight crevices when hunting.

BETTA FISH

The Betta Fish, also called Siamese Fighting Fish, is a small, colorful freshwater fish known for its flowing fins and vibrant colors. Bettas typically grow up to 3in (7.6cm) in length and weigh around 0.09–0.1oz (2.5–3g). They can swim at a speed of about 2.2mph (3.5kph). Bettas are omnivores, feeding on insects, larvae and plant matter. These territorial fish are often kept in aquariums due to their striking appearance and captivating behavior. They belong to the class, ***Actinopterygii*** and the ***Osphronemidae*** family. Their scientific name is ***Betta splendens***.

DID YOU KNOW?

Betta Fish are capable of recognizing their owners and can learn simple tricks.

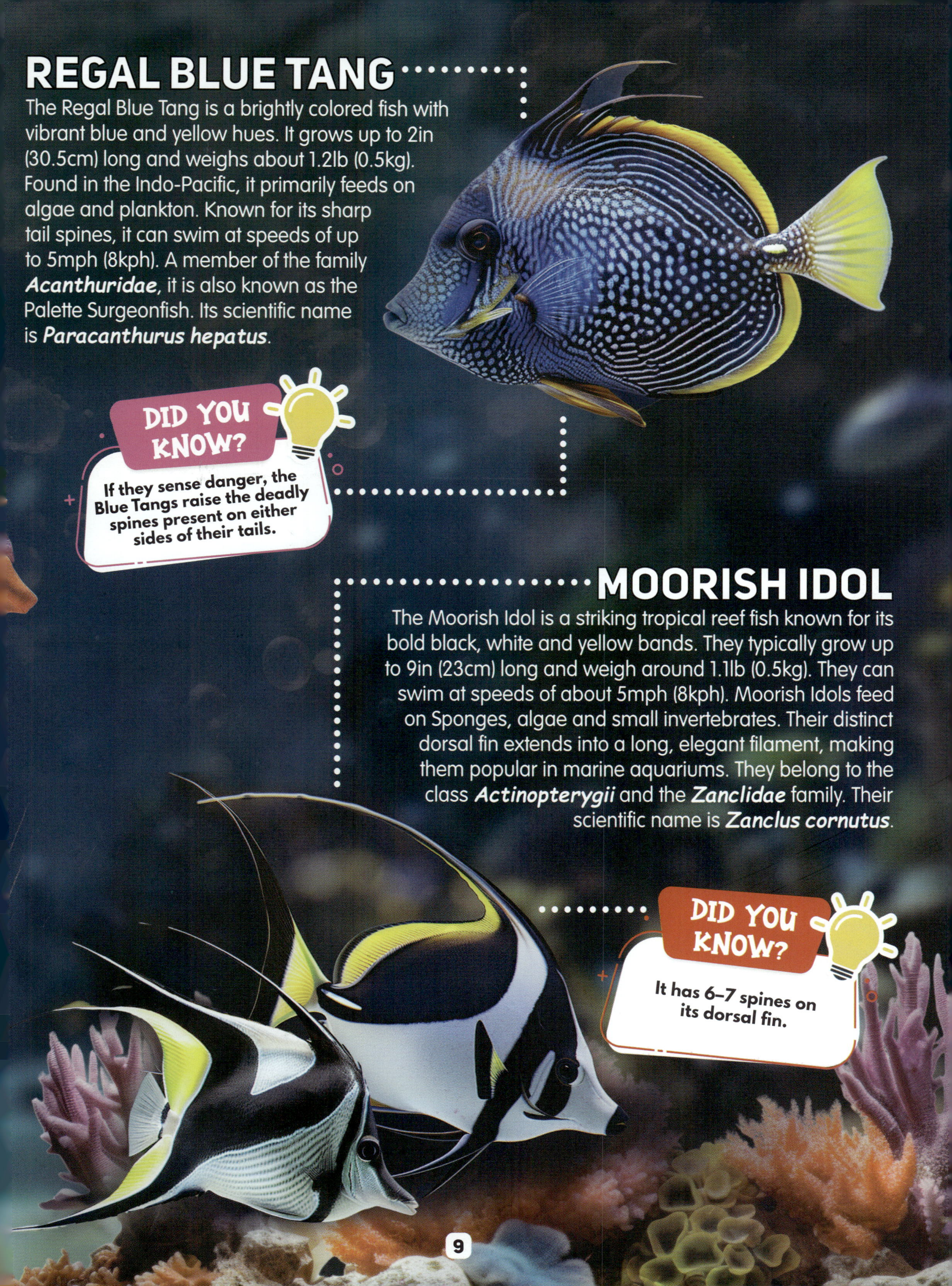

REGAL BLUE TANG

The Regal Blue Tang is a brightly colored fish with vibrant blue and yellow hues. It grows up to 2in (30.5cm) long and weighs about 1.2lb (0.5kg). Found in the Indo-Pacific, it primarily feeds on algae and plankton. Known for its sharp tail spines, it can swim at speeds of up to 5mph (8kph). A member of the family ***Acanthuridae***, it is also known as the Palette Surgeonfish. Its scientific name is ***Paracanthurus hepatus***.

DID YOU KNOW?

If they sense danger, the Blue Tangs raise the deadly spines present on either sides of their tails.

MOORISH IDOL

The Moorish Idol is a striking tropical reef fish known for its bold black, white and yellow bands. They typically grow up to 9in (23cm) long and weigh around 1.1lb (0.5kg). They can swim at speeds of about 5mph (8kph). Moorish Idols feed on Sponges, algae and small invertebrates. Their distinct dorsal fin extends into a long, elegant filament, making them popular in marine aquariums. They belong to the class ***Actinopterygii*** and the ***Zanclidae*** family. Their scientific name is ***Zanclus cornutus***.

DID YOU KNOW?

It has 6–7 spines on its dorsal fin.

MANDARIN FISH

The Mandarin Fish is a small, vibrant reef fish known for its striking blue, orange and green patterns. This fish typically grows to about 2.4in (6cm) long and weighs less than 1oz (28g). It is a slow swimmer, gliding gracefully through coral reefs. Mandarin Fish feed on small crustaceans, Copepods and Amphipods. It belongs to the class ***Actinopterygii*** and the family ***Callionymidae***. Its scientific name, ***Synchiropus splendidus***, reflects its splendid appearance.

DID YOU KNOW?

Mandarin Fish have mildly toxic skin and mucus, which deters predators.

EMPEROR ANGELFISH

The Emperor Angelfish is a stunning reef fish known for its vibrant blue and yellow stripes and bold black mask over its eyes. This fish can grow up to 15in (38cm) long and weighs around 3lb (1.4kg). It feeds on Sponges, algae and small invertebrates. With a swimming speed of about 2mph (3.2kph), it inhabits coral reefs across the Indo-Pacific region. It belongs to the class ***Actinopterygii*** and the family ***Pomacanthidae***. Its scientific name is ***Pomacanthus imperator***.

DID YOU KNOW?

Emperor Angelfish are territorial, defending their space against other fish species.

LIONFISH

The Lionfish is a striking marine predator known for its long, venomous spines and vibrant stripes of red, white and brown. It has a body length of 12–15in (30.5–38cm) and can weigh up to 2.6lb (1.2kg). Despite its slow swimming speed of around 5mph (8kph), it is a skilled hunter. Lionfish feeds on small fish, crustaceans and mollusks. It belongs to the class ***Actinopterygii*** and the family ***Scorpaenidae***. The scientific name of the Red Lionfish is ***Pterois volitans***, making them a beautiful yet invasive species in many oceans.

DID YOU KNOW?

Lionfish are invasive species living in the non-native Atlantic ocean and causing harm to its reef ecosystem.

CLOWNFISH

The Clownfish is a small, brightly colored fish found in coral reefs. They typically grow up to 4in (10cm) long and weigh about 7oz (198g). Their bodies are orange with white bands outlined in black. They can swim at speeds of around 2mph (3.2kph). These fish form a symbiotic relationship with Sea Anemones, where they find shelter and protection. Clownfish are omnivores, eating algae, plankton and small invertebrates, such as Zooplankton and crustaceans. Clownfish belong to the family ***Pomacentridae***. The scientific name of Clownfish is ***Amphiprioninae ocellaris***.

DID YOU KNOW?

All Clownfish are born male. When the dominant female dies, the dominant male turns turn itself into a female.

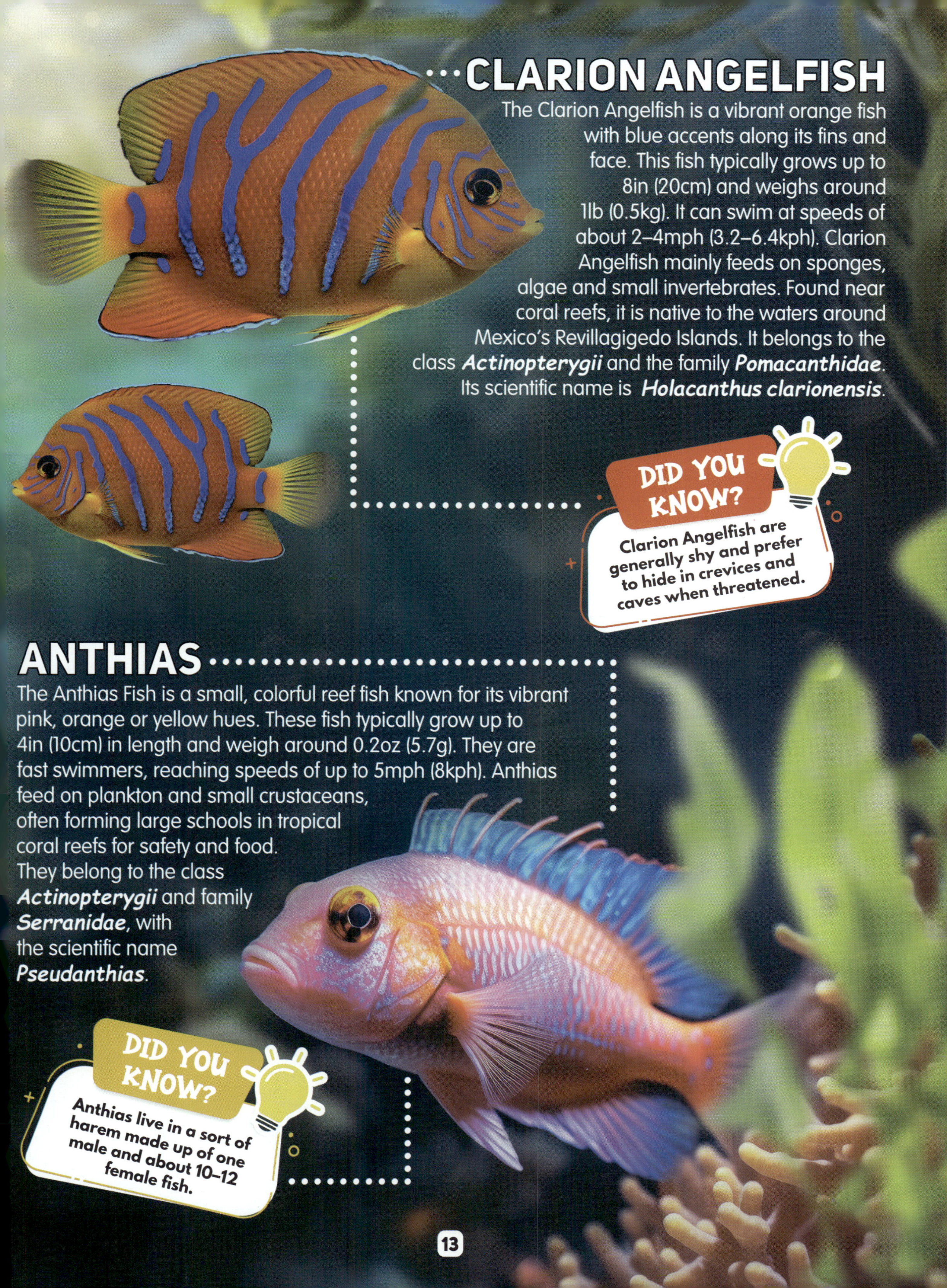

CLARION ANGELFISH

The Clarion Angelfish is a vibrant orange fish with blue accents along its fins and face. This fish typically grows up to 8in (20cm) and weighs around 1lb (0.5kg). It can swim at speeds of about 2–4mph (3.2–6.4kph). Clarion Angelfish mainly feeds on sponges, algae and small invertebrates. Found near coral reefs, it is native to the waters around Mexico's Revillagigedo Islands. It belongs to the class ***Actinopterygii*** and the family ***Pomacanthidae***. Its scientific name is ***Holacanthus clarionensis***.

DID YOU KNOW?

Clarion Angelfish are generally shy and prefer to hide in crevices and caves when threatened.

ANTHIAS

The Anthias Fish is a small, colorful reef fish known for its vibrant pink, orange or yellow hues. These fish typically grow up to 4in (10cm) in length and weigh around 0.2oz (5.7g). They are fast swimmers, reaching speeds of up to 5mph (8kph). Anthias feed on plankton and small crustaceans, often forming large schools in tropical coral reefs for safety and food. They belong to the class ***Actinopterygii*** and family ***Serranidae***, with the scientific name ***Pseudanthias***.

DID YOU KNOW?

Anthias live in a sort of harem made up of one male and about 10–12 female fish.

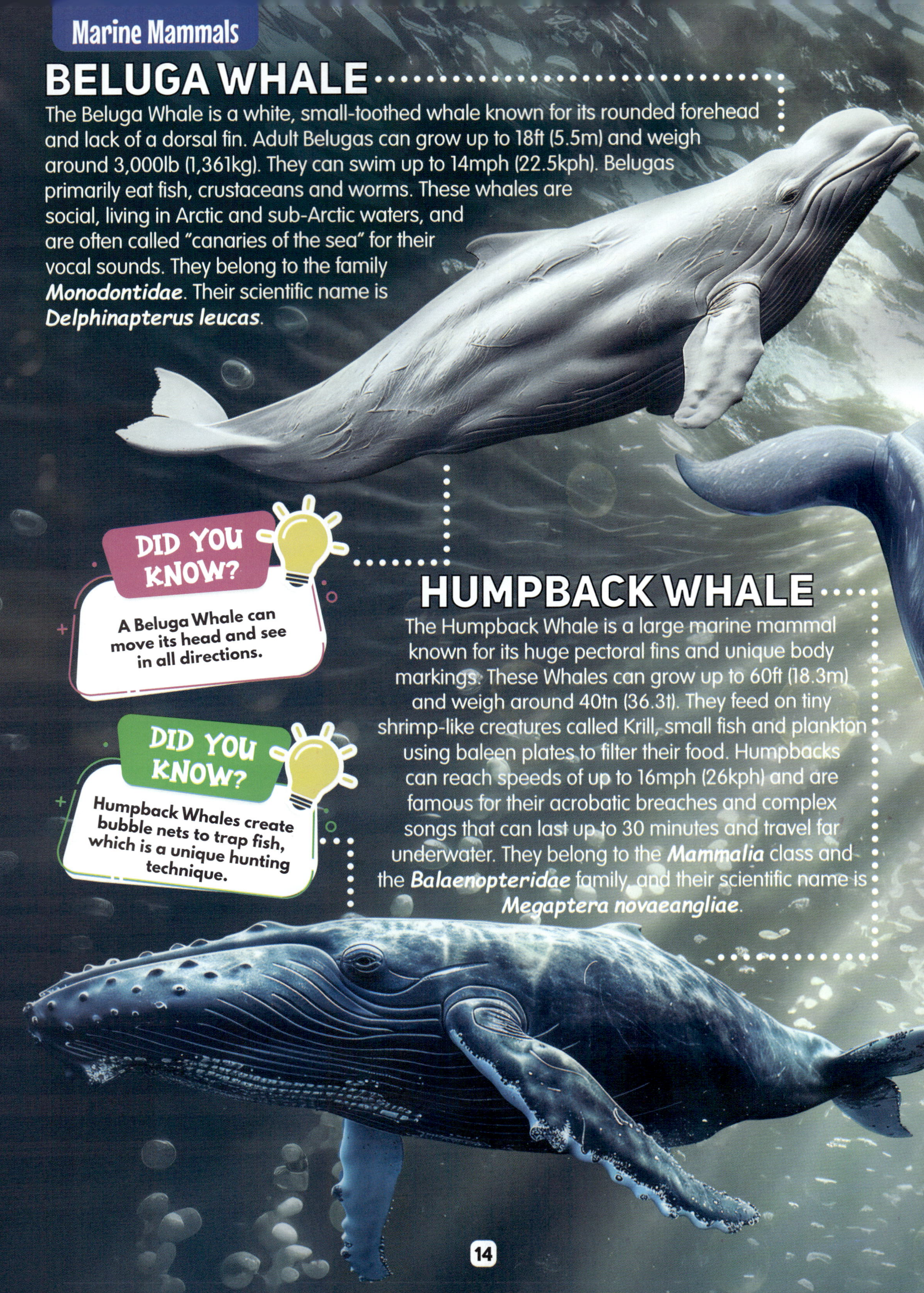

BELUGA WHALE

The Beluga Whale is a white, small-toothed whale known for its rounded forehead and lack of a dorsal fin. Adult Belugas can grow up to 18ft (5.5m) and weigh around 3,000lb (1,361kg). They can swim up to 14mph (22.5kph). Belugas primarily eat fish, crustaceans and worms. These whales are social, living in Arctic and sub-Arctic waters, and are often called "canaries of the sea" for their vocal sounds. They belong to the family ***Monodontidae***. Their scientific name is ***Delphinapterus leucas***.

DID YOU KNOW?

A Beluga Whale can move its head and see in all directions.

DID YOU KNOW?

Humpback Whales create bubble nets to trap fish, which is a unique hunting technique.

HUMPBACK WHALE

The Humpback Whale is a large marine mammal known for its huge pectoral fins and unique body markings. These Whales can grow up to 60ft (18.3m) and weigh around 40tn (36.3t). They feed on tiny shrimp-like creatures called Krill, small fish and plankton using baleen plates to filter their food. Humpbacks can reach speeds of up to 16mph (26kph) and are famous for their acrobatic breaches and complex songs that can last up to 30 minutes and travel far underwater. They belong to the ***Mammalia*** class and the ***Balaenopteridae*** family, and their scientific name is ***Megaptera novaeangliae***.

BLUE WHALE

The Blue Whale is the largest animal on Earth. These gentle giants can grow up to 100ft (30.5m) long and weigh around 200tn (181t). Their sleek, streamlined bodies help them reach speeds of up to 20mph (32kph). Blue Whales feed primarily on Krill, consuming tons daily during feeding seasons. They have a heart the size of a small car and live in oceans worldwide, migrating between feeding and breeding grounds. They belong to the family ***Balaenopteridae***. Their scientific name is ***Balaenoptera musculus***.

DID YOU KNOW?

The tongue of a Blue Whale weighs approximately equal to the weight of an Elephant.

SEAL

The Seal is a marine mammal with a streamlined body, flippers and thick blubber to keep it warm in cold waters. They range in size from 3–20ft (0.9–6m) and weigh around 100–8,800lb (45–3,992kg), depending on the species. Seals can swim up to 25mph (40kph) and primarily feed on fish, Squid and crustaceans. There are two types of Seals—earless and eared. The earless belong to the ***Phocidae*** family while the eared ones to the ***Otariidae***. Their scientific name is ***Pinnipedia***.

DID YOU KNOW?

Seals can hold their breath for long periods, up to 30 minutes, when diving for food.

MANATEE

The Manatee is a large, gentle marine mammal known as "sea cow." Manatees have a rounded body covered in gray or brown skin, with paddle-like front flippers and a wide, flat tail that helps them glide through the water. They can grow up to 13ft (4m) long and weigh around 1,200lb (544kg). They are slow swimmers, reaching speeds of only 3–5mph (4.8–8kph). Manatees are herbivores, feeding on seagrass, algae and other aquatic plants in shallow coastal waters. They belong to the family ***Trichechidae***, with 3 species varying according to their habitat. The scientific name of Manatees is ***Trichechus***.

DOLPHIN

The Dolphin is a sleek marine mammal known for its streamlined body and exceptional swimming ability. They weigh around 600–12,000lb (272–5,443kg) and can grow about 32ft (9.8m) long. Dolphins can reach speeds of up to 18mph (29kph). They primarily feed on fish and Squid. Dolphins belong to the class ***Mammalia*** and the family ***Delphinidae***. Their scientific name varies according to the species. The scientific name of the well-known Bottlenose Dolphin is ***Tursiops truncatus***.

SEA OTTER

The Sea Otter is a large marine mammal known for its dense fur and playful nature. They weigh around 30–100lb (14–45kg) and can grow up to 5ft (1.5m) long. Sea Otters primarily feed on marine invertebrates like Sea Urchins, Crabs and Clams. They are agile swimmers, reaching speeds of 5.6mph (9kph). Sea Otters are vital to marine ecosystems, maintaining kelp forest health. They inhabit coastal waters in the northern Pacific Ocean. Classified in the class ***Mammalia*** and the family ***Mustelidae***, their scientific name is ***Enhydra lutris***.

DID YOU KNOW?

90 percent of the Sea Otters reside in coastal Alaska.

DID YOU KNOW?

They spend most of their time out of the water on logs and rocks, socializing.

STELLER SEA LION

The Steller Sea Lion is the largest of sea lions, with males reaching up to 12ft (3.6m) long and weighing over 2,400lb (1,089kg). These mammals are known for their large size, robust body and golden-brown fur. They primarily feed on fish, Squid and Octopuses. Steller Sea Lions are capable of swimming at speeds of 25mph (40kph). They belong to the family ***Otariidae***, and are found along the coasts of the North Pacific. Their scientific name is ***Eumetopias jubatus***.

WALRUS

The Walrus is a large marine mammal found in the Arctic and sub-Arctic regions. They can grow up to 12ft (3.6m) long and weigh as much as 2,000lb (907kg). Walruses have thick skin and long tusks, which they use for hauling themselves onto ice and during fighting. They are strong swimmers, reaching speeds of up to 22mph (35kph) in short bursts. They feed on Mussels, benthic invertebrates, Clams, etc. Walruses belong to the class ***Mammalia*** and the family ***Odobenidae***, playing a vital role in Arctic ecosystems. Their scientific name is ***Odobenus rosmarus***.

DID YOU KNOW?

The tusks of a walrus can measure as long as 35in (90cm).

BOBTAIL SQUID

The Bobtail Squid is a small marine animal with a rounded body and large, expressive eyes. It has a unique, shimmering appearance due to bioluminescent bacteria in its mantle, which help it camouflage. This tiny squid grows up to 2in (5cm). It has a very short lifespan of 3–10 months and feeds on small crustaceans and plankton at night. Belonging to the class ***Cephalopoda*** and the family ***Sepiolidae***, the scientific name of Hawaiian Bobtail Squid is ***Euprymna scolopes***.

DID YOU KNOW?

Bobtail Squids can change their color and texture to blend with the seafloor.

DID YOU KNOW?

Anglerfish have a fishing-rod like spine protruding from their snout that helps them catch their prey.

ANGLERFISH

The Anglerfish is a deep-sea predator known for its glowing lure, which it uses to attract prey in the dark ocean depths. This fish can grow up to 3.3ft (1m) long and weigh around 110lb (50kg). Anglerfish has sharp teeth and a large mouth to consume prey like small fish and crustaceans. Despite its eerie appearance, it is a slow swimmer, reaching speeds of just 0.2mph (0.3kph). It belongs to the order ***Lophiiformes***. The scientific name of Deep-Sea Anglerfish is ***Ceratias holboelli***.

GIANT SQUID

The Giant Squid is one of the largest invertebrates on Earth. They can grow up to 43ft (13m) long and weigh up to 1,000lb (454kg). Their body features large eyes, measuring up to 10in (25cm), that help them see in the deep ocean's darkness. Giant squids have 8 arms and 2 longer tentacles lined with suction cups for capturing prey. They feed on fish, other Squids and deep-sea creatures. Despite their size, they can reach speeds of up to 25mph (40kph). They belong to the class ***Cephalopoda*** and the family ***Architeuthidae***. Scientific name of the Giant Squids is ***Architeuthis dux***.

DID YOU KNOW?

The largest of the Giant Squids ever recorded was 59ft (18m) in length.

GIANT PACIFIC OCTOPUS

The Giant Pacific Octopus is the largest octopus species, found in the deep cold waters. It inhabits rocky crevices and ocean floors up to 6,600ft (2,000m) deep. This octopus can grow up to 16ft (5m) and weighs over 110lb (50kg). Its soft, bulbous body allows it to squeeze through small spaces, while its 8 arms, lined with powerful suction cups, help catch prey. It feeds on Crabs, Clams, fish and even small Sharks. This Octopus is known for its intelligence and can change color and texture to blend with its surroundings. Despite its large size, it can swim at speeds of up to 25mph (40kph). It belongs to the class ***Cephalopoda*** and the family ***Octopodidae***. Its scientific name is ***Enteroctopus dofleini***.

DID YOU KNOW?

Giant Pacific Octopus are intelligent and have proven to solve mazes in scientific tests.

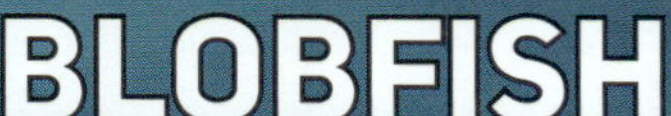

BLOBFISH

The Blobfish is a deep-sea fish known for its jelly-like, blob-like appearance when brought to the surface. It typically grows up to 1ft (0.3m) long and weighs around 4lb (1.8kg). Living at depths of 2,000–4,000ft (610–1219m), it has a soft, gelatinous body that helps it withstand immense pressure. Blobfish feeds on small crustaceans and deep-sea invertebrates. It belongs to the family ***Psychrolutidae***. Its scientific name is ***Psychrolutes marcidus***.

DID YOU KNOW?

At the water surface, the blobfish collapses into a floppy mass due to less pressure.

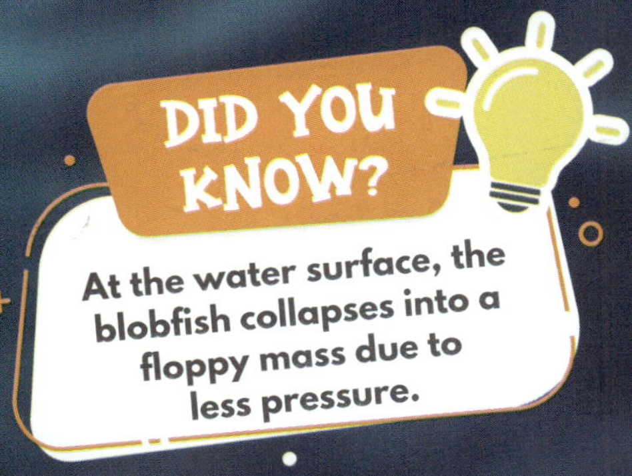

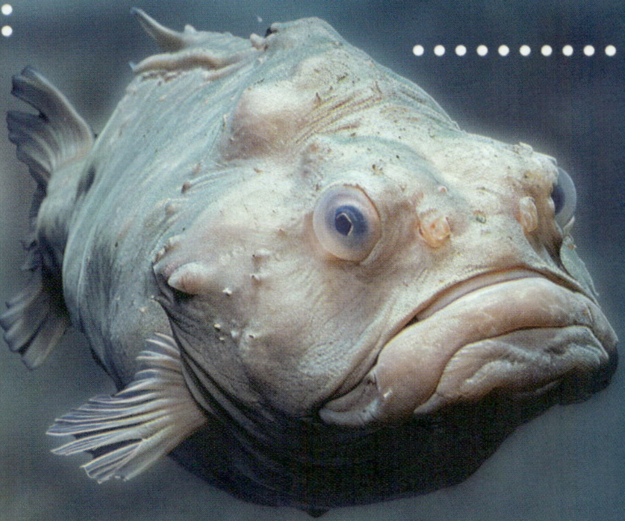

BLUE-RINGED OCTOPUS

The Blue-Ringed Octopus is a small but highly venomous deep-sea creature. Found at depths of up to 164ft (50m), it inhabits coral reefs and tide pools. This octopus grows up to 8in (20cm) and weighs around 1oz (28g). It displays bright blue rings when threatened. It feeds on small crustaceans, Shrimp and fish, using venom to immobilize prey. Despite its small size, it can swim at speeds of 4mph (6kph). It belongs to the class ***Cephalopoda*** and the family ***Octopodidae***. It belongs to the genus ***Hapalochlaena***.

DID YOU KNOW?

Its venomous bite is fatal to a human.

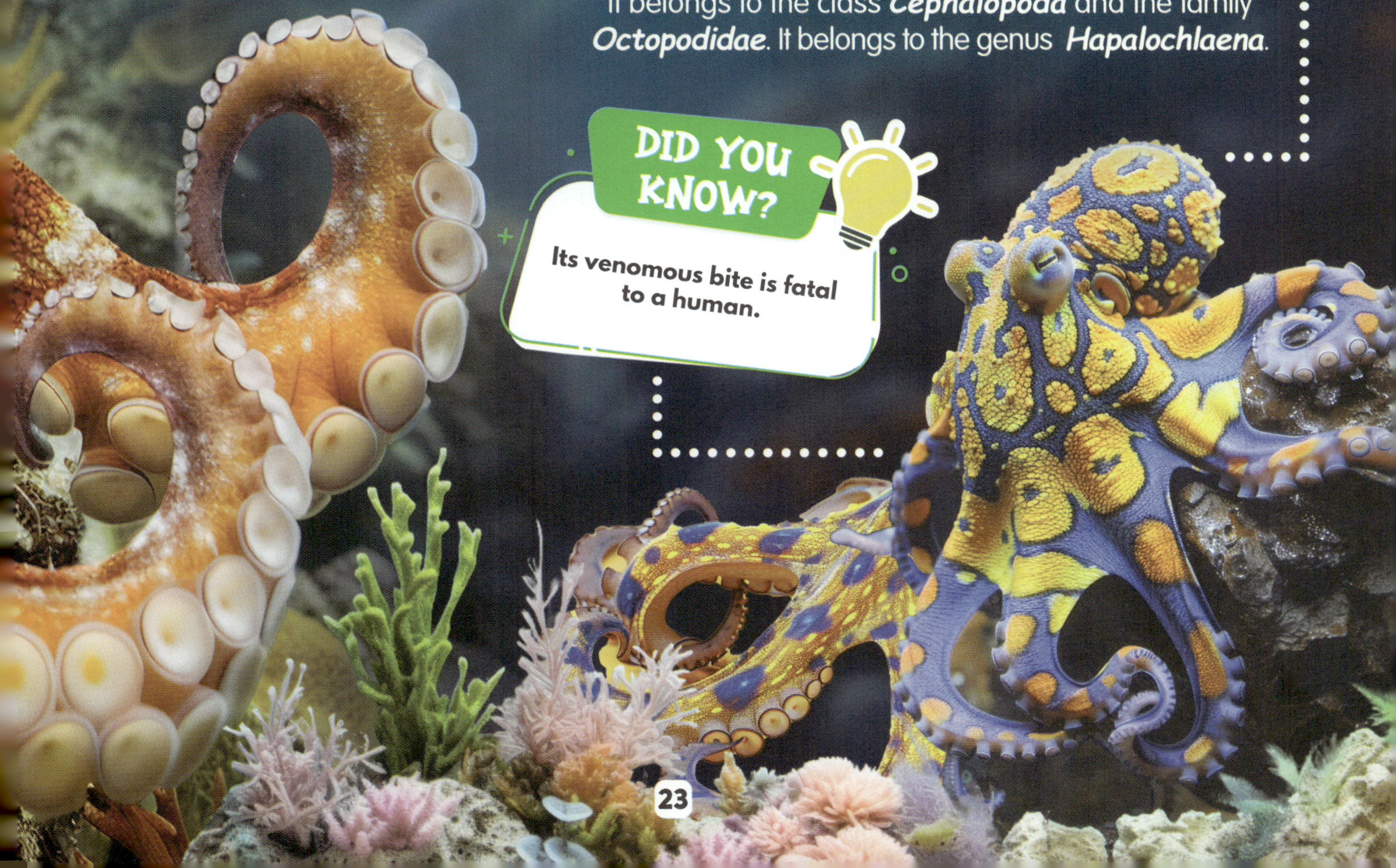

RIBBON EEL

The Ribbon Eel is a colorful marine eel known for its striking blue and yellow coloration. They grow up to 3.3ft (1m) long and weigh around 1.5lb (0.7kg). These Eels are found in coral reefs, where they feed on small fish and invertebrates. Ribbon Eels are fast swimmers, using their agility to capture prey. They belong to the class ***Actinopterygii*** and the family ***Muraenidae***, and are native to the Indo-Pacific region. Their scientific name is ***Rhinomuraena quaesita***.

DID YOU KNOW?

Ribbon Eels stay in the same cave for months or even years.

MORAY EEL

The Moray Eel is a long, snake-like fish found in warm, shallow waters. Moray Eels can grow up to 13ft (4m) long and weigh around 30lb (14kg). They have a slender, muscular body with sharp teeth, which they use to catch prey. Morays are not fast swimmers but are excellent ambush predators, hiding in crevices. They belong to the class ***Actinopterygii*** and are common in tropical and subtropical oceans. It is a member of the ***Muraenidae*** family.

DID YOU KNOW?

In some parts people eat the Moray but its skin can be toxic.

ELECTRIC EEL

The Electric Eel is a fascinating fish known for its ability to generate powerful electric shocks. It can grow up to 8ft (2.4m) long and weigh around 44lb (20kg). It moves slowly, reaching speeds of about 3mph (4.8kph). Despite its name, it's not technically an Eel but a Knifefish. Its elongated, cylindrical body allows it to glide through the water with minimal resistance. The Electric Eel uses its shock to stun prey like fish, amphibians and small mammals. It can generate up to 600V of electricity. The Electric Eel belongs to the class ***Actinopterygii*** and family ***Gymnotidae***. Its scientific name is ***Electrophorus electricus***.

DID YOU KNOW?

Electric Eels appear like Eels and are named so, when in real they are related to carp.

BANDED SEA KRAIT

The Banded Sea Krait is a highly venomous Sea Snake found in the Indo-Pacific region. They have a slender, elongated body, with distinct black and white bands that give them their name. Adults can grow up to 6.6ft (2m) long and weigh around 1.1lb (0.5kg). These Snakes are excellent swimmers and can move at speeds of up to 1.5mph (2.4kph). Banded Sea Kraits feed primarily on fish and Eels, diving underwater to hunt. Despite their venom, they are generally not aggressive. They are part of the class ***Reptilia*** and family ***Elapidae***. Scientific name for the Banded Sea Kraits is ***Laticauda colubrina***.

DID YOU KNOW?

Banded Sea Kraits come to land to lay their eggs.

PIPEFISH

The Pipefish is a slender, elongated fish resembling a small, narrow pipe. Typically reaching lengths of 7–15in (17.8–38cm), they have a long, tubular body and a small, horse-like head. Pipefish are slow swimmers and are often found in seagrass beds or coral reefs. They feed on small crustaceans and plankton. These fish belong to the family ***Syngnathidae***, with over 200 species worldwide. Scientific name for the Yellow-Banded Pipefish is ***Dunckerocampus pessuliferus***.

DID YOU KNOW?

Pipefish don't have a stomach, so they must eat constantly to stay nourished.

DID YOU KNOW?

They hide in rock crevices and emerge out at night to hunt.

DRAGON MORAY EEL

The Dragon Moray Eel is a striking species found in the Indo-Pacific. They grow up to 3.3ft (1m) in length and can weigh around 10lb (4.5kg). With their dragon-like appearance, they have a long, slender body and a distinctive pattern. Dragon Moray Eels primarily feed on fish and crustaceans. They are known for their agility and can swim swiftly. Belonging to the family ***Muraenidae***, they inhabit coral reefs and rocky areas. Their scientific name is ***Enchelycore pardalis***.

HERMIT CRAB

The Hermit Crab is a unique crustacean that uses empty shells for protection. They have a soft, coiled abdomen that fits snugly inside shells, and strong claws for defense and climbing. Hermit Crabs range in size from 0.5–16in (1.3–40.6cm) and can weigh up to 11lb (5kg) in larger species. They feed on algae, plankton and organic debris. Belonging to the class ***Malacostraca*** and the family ***Paguroidea***, they move at a slow pace and thrive in coastal and marine habitats.

DID YOU KNOW?

They are not true Crabs as they use deserted shells of other animals and are related to Lobsters.

FIDDLER CRAB

The Fiddler Crab is a small crustacean known for its asymmetrical claws, with males sporting one oversized claw used for communication and defense. They measure up to 2in (5cm) across and weigh less than 1oz (28g). These crabs feed on algae and organic debris, sifting through sand or mud with their smaller claw. Fiddler Crabs can live, at the most, for 2 years. Found in intertidal zones, they thrive in sandy or muddy habitats. They belong to the class ***Malacostraca*** and family ***Ocypodidae***. They are one of the many species of the genus ***Uca***.

DID YOU KNOW?

Fiddler Crabs dig burrows to feed on organic matter and for protection.

JAPANESE SPIDER CRAB

The Japanese Spider Crab is the largest crab species, known for its long, spindly legs. Their leg span can reach up to 12ft (3.7m), and they can weigh as much as 44lb (20kg). Their body is orange with white spots. These slow-moving crabs inhabit deep waters around Japan and are scavengers, feeding on dead animals, Shellfish and plant matter. Belonging to the class ***Malacostraca*** and the family ***Inachidae***, they are fascinating creatures adapted to life on the seafloor. Scientific name for the Japanese Spider Crabs is ***Macrocheira kaempferi***.

DID YOU KNOW?

A Japanese Spider Crab's legs can grow up to 12ft (3.7m) in length, larger than 2 fully grown men.

AMERICAN LOBSTER

The American Lobster is a marine crustacean with a hard, reddish-brown exoskeleton that can turn bright red when cooked. They have a robust body, large claws for crushing and cutting and a tail that aids in swimming. Adult Lobsters can grow up to 3.25ft (0.99m) long, weigh up to 44lb (20kg), and can move at speeds of about 11mph (18kph) in short bursts. They are omnivores, feeding on fish, mollusks, algae and detritus found on the ocean floor. They belong to the class ***Malacostraca*** and the family ***Nephropidae***. The scientific name of American Lobster is ***Homarus americanus***.

DID YOU KNOW?

They shed their shells to grow and can age to 50 years and even more.

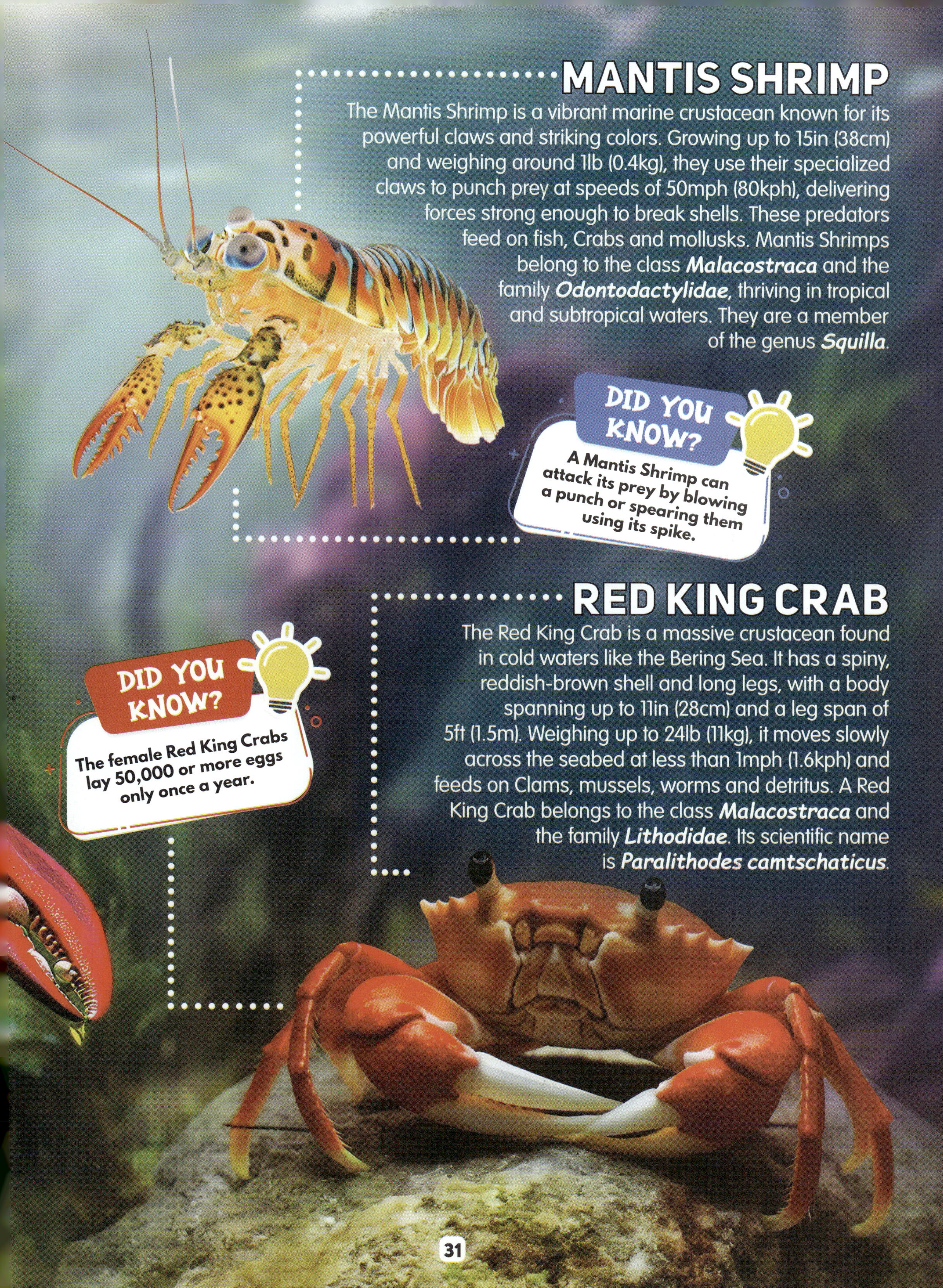

MANTIS SHRIMP

The Mantis Shrimp is a vibrant marine crustacean known for its powerful claws and striking colors. Growing up to 15in (38cm) and weighing around 1lb (0.4kg), they use their specialized claws to punch prey at speeds of 50mph (80kph), delivering forces strong enough to break shells. These predators feed on fish, Crabs and mollusks. Mantis Shrimps belong to the class ***Malacostraca*** and the family ***Odontodactylidae***, thriving in tropical and subtropical waters. They are a member of the genus ***Squilla***.

DID YOU KNOW?

A Mantis Shrimp can attack its prey by blowing a punch or spearing them using its spike.

RED KING CRAB

The Red King Crab is a massive crustacean found in cold waters like the Bering Sea. It has a spiny, reddish-brown shell and long legs, with a body spanning up to 11in (28cm) and a leg span of 5ft (1.5m). Weighing up to 24lb (11kg), it moves slowly across the seabed at less than 1mph (1.6kph) and feeds on Clams, mussels, worms and detritus. A Red King Crab belongs to the class ***Malacostraca*** and the family ***Lithodidae***. Its scientific name is ***Paralithodes camtschaticus***.

DID YOU KNOW?

The female Red King Crabs lay 50,000 or more eggs only once a year.

SWORDFISH

The Swordfish is a large, powerful fish known for its long, flattened bill, which resembles a sword. Their bill is used to slash through schools of fish, their primary food source, including Squid and smaller fish. Swordfish can grow up to 10ft (3m) long and weigh as much as 1,200lb (544kg). They are fast swimmers, reaching speeds of up to 50mph (80kph). Found in warm ocean waters, they are solitary and migratory creatures, spending much of their time in deep waters. Swordfish belong to the class ***Actinopterygii*** and the family ***Xiphiidae***. Scientific name for the swordfish is ***Xiphias gladius***.

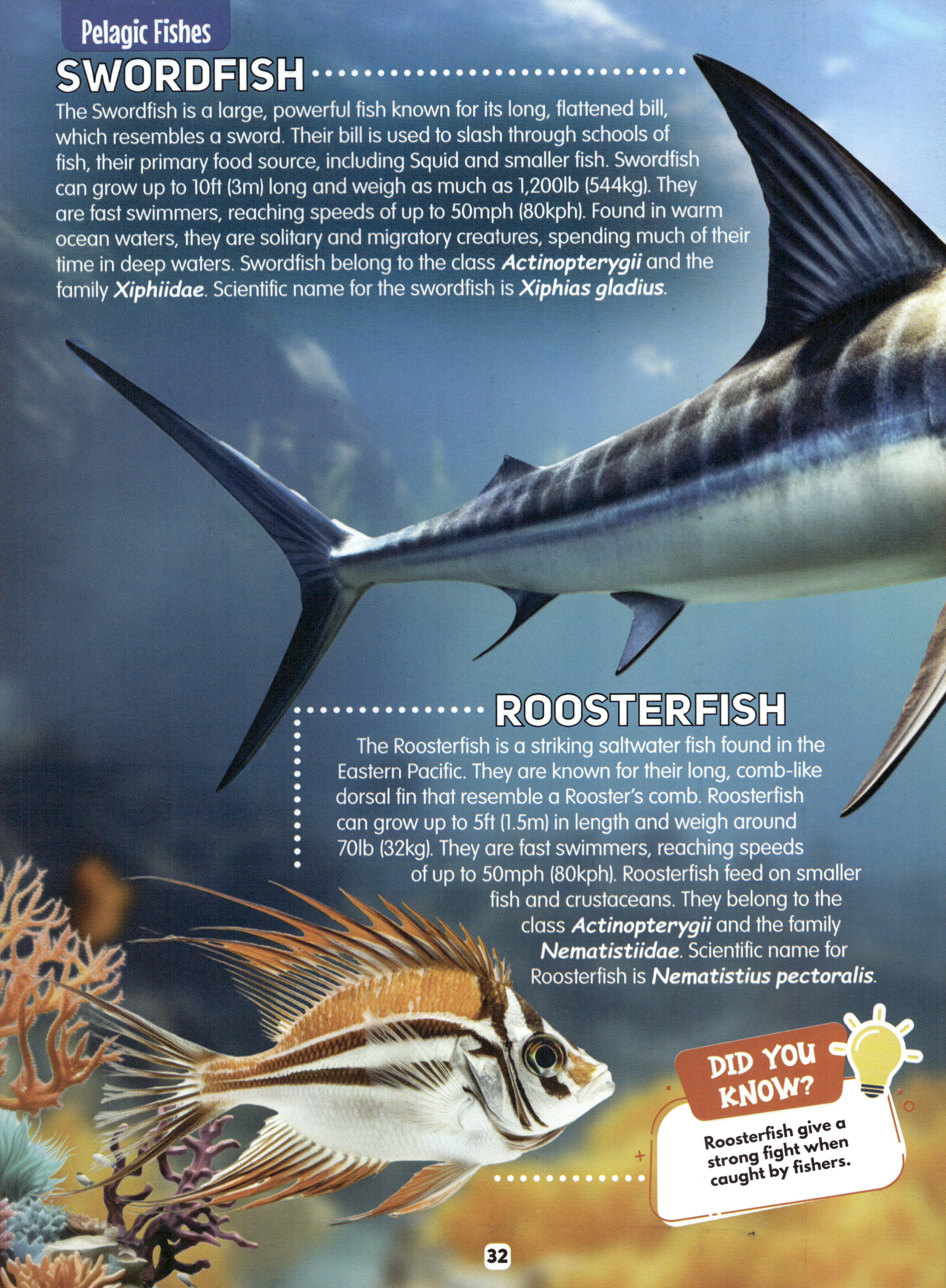

ROOSTERFISH

The Roosterfish is a striking saltwater fish found in the Eastern Pacific. They are known for their long, comb-like dorsal fin that resemble a Rooster's comb. Roosterfish can grow up to 5ft (1.5m) in length and weigh around 70lb (32kg). They are fast swimmers, reaching speeds of up to 50mph (80kph). Roosterfish feed on smaller fish and crustaceans. They belong to the class ***Actinopterygii*** and the family ***Nematistiidae***. Scientific name for Roosterfish is ***Nematistius pectoralis***.

DID YOU KNOW?

Roosterfish give a strong fight when caught by fishers.

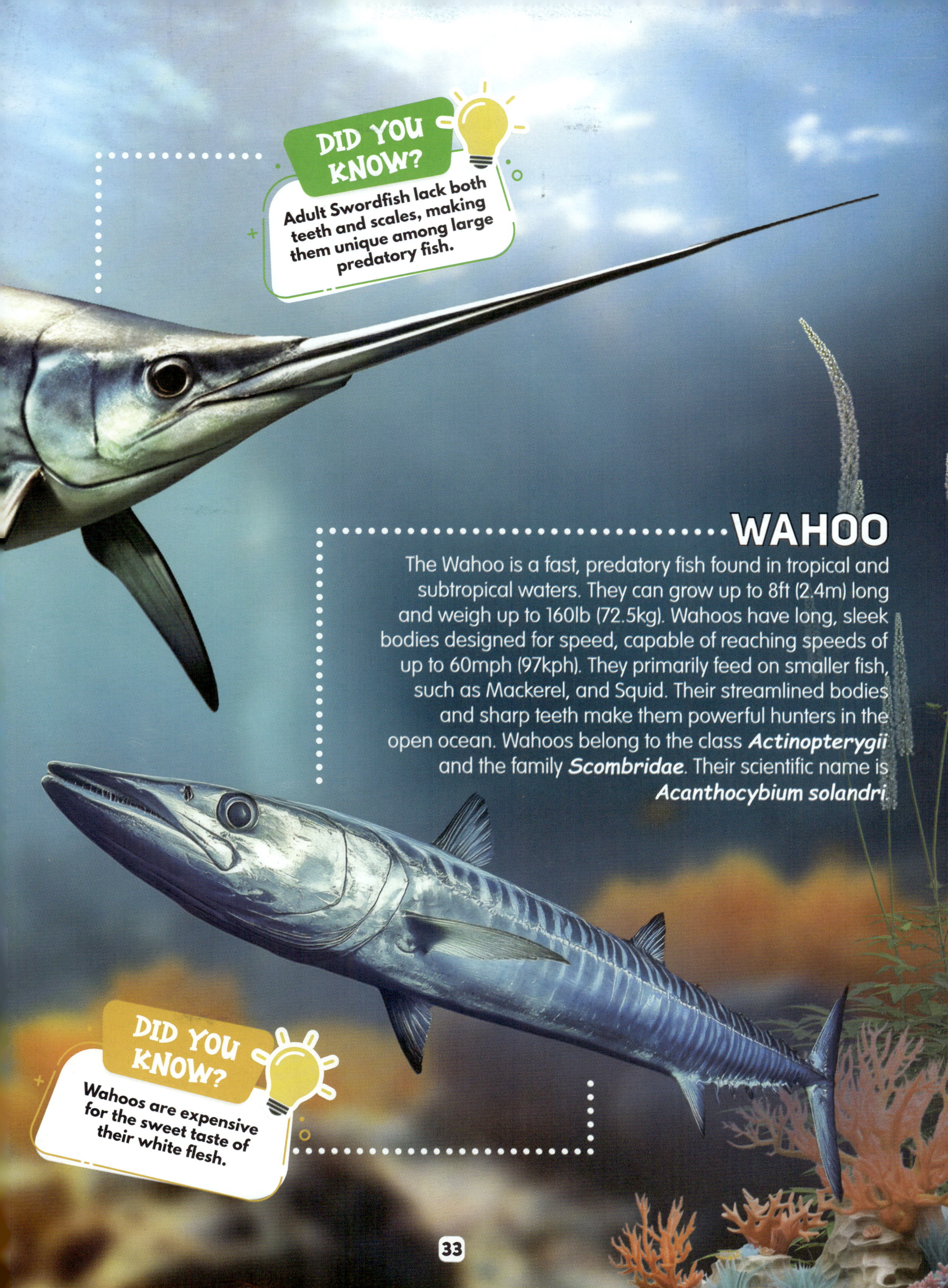

DID YOU KNOW?

Adult Swordfish lack both teeth and scales, making them unique among large predatory fish.

WAHOO

The Wahoo is a fast, predatory fish found in tropical and subtropical waters. They can grow up to 8ft (2.4m) long and weigh up to 160lb (72.5kg). Wahoos have long, sleek bodies designed for speed, capable of reaching speeds of up to 60mph (97kph). They primarily feed on smaller fish, such as Mackerel, and Squid. Their streamlined bodies and sharp teeth make them powerful hunters in the open ocean. Wahoos belong to the class ***Actinopterygii*** and the family ***Scombridae***. Their scientific name is ***Acanthocybium solandri***.

DID YOU KNOW?

Wahoos are expensive for the sweet taste of their white flesh.

BLUE MARLIN

The Blue Marlin is a powerful and fast-swimming fish known for its long, sharp bill and cobalt-blue coloring with a silver belly. They can grow up to 14ft (4.3m) and weigh over 1,800lb (816kg), although most are smaller. Blue Marlins can travel long distances of about 1,000mi (1,609km) with great speed. They feed on Squid, Mackerel, Tuna and other small fish. They inhabit warm, tropical and subtropical oceans. Their size, speed and elegance make them a prized species for sport fishing. Belonging to family ***Istiophoridae***, their scientific name is ***Makaira igricans***.

DID YOU KNOW?

Blue Marlin leaves its eggs afloat in open water and provides no care.

SAILFISH

The Sailfish is known for its impressive sail-like dorsal fin and sleek, elongated body. They can grow above 10ft (3m) in length and weigh up to 200lb (91kg). Sailfish are incredibly fast swimmers, reaching speeds of up to 68mph (109kph), making them one of the fastest fish in the world. They primarily feed on smaller fish and Squid. Their distinctive sail is used for stability while swimming at high speeds. Sailfish belong to the family ***Istiophoridae*** and the genus ***Istiophorus***.

DID YOU KNOW?

It is one of the most sought-after fish and thus have an average lifespan of only 4 years.

TARPON

The Tarpon is a large fish known for its silver scales and elongated body. They can grow up to 6ft (1.8m) long and weigh 100lb (45kg) and more. Tarpons are powerful swimmers, reaching speeds of up to 35mph (56kph). They are primarily carnivorous, feeding on fish, crustaceans and small invertebrates. Found in warm coastal waters, they belong to the class ***Actinopterygii*** and the family ***Megalopidae***. The scientific name of the Atlantic Tarpon is ***Megalops atlanticus***.

DID YOU KNOW?

Due to its majestic appearance, the Tarpon is nicknamed "silver king."

COMMON CARP

The Common Carp is a large freshwater fish known for its adaptability and importance in aquaculture. They have a robust body covered with large, shiny scales and can grow up to 2ft (0.6m) long, weighing up to 66lb (30kg). These fish are omnivorous, feeding on plants, insects and small invertebrates. Common Carp can swim at speeds of up to 5mph (8kph). Native to Europe and Asia, they thrive in calm, warm waters. They belong to the class ***Actinopterygii*** and the family ***Cyprinidae***. Their scientific name is ***Cyprinus carpio***.

DID YOU KNOW?

Common Carp grow quickly, especially in nutrient-rich waters.

STONEFISH

The Stonefish is one of the most venomous fish in the world, found in tropical marine waters. Their rough, camouflaged body resembles a rock, helping them ambush prey. Stonefish grow up to 20in (51 cm) long and weigh about 5lb (2.3kg). They are slow-moving but can strike prey, like small fish and crustaceans, in milliseconds. They also use venomous spines for defense against predators. Belonging to the class ***Actinopterygii*** and the family ***Synanceiidae***, their scientific name is ***Synanceia verrucosa***.

DID YOU KNOW?

Stonefish have about 13 dorsal fin spines that they may raise in self-defense.

CATFISH

The Catfish is a diverse group of fish known for their whisker-like barbels around the mouth. They can vary greatly in size, ranging from small species of a few inches to giants which can grow up to 15ft (4.6m) and weigh over 600lb (272kg). Catfish are bottom dwellers and use their barbels to sense food, such as smaller fish, crustaceans and plant matter. They are relatively slow swimmers. Found around the globe, most species live in freshwater. Catfish belong to the order ***Siluriformes***.

DID YOU KNOW?

A Catfish's entire body is covered with taste buds that can detect chemicals in the water and respond to touch.

SCORPION FISH

The Scorpionfish is a venomous marine fish known for its spiny fins and camouflaged appearance that blends with coral and rocky seafloors. They grow up to 39in (99cm) and weigh around 3.3lb (1.5kg). Scorpionfish are ambush predators, feeding on small fish and crustaceans. They remain motionless, striking prey with surprising speed, though their swimming speed is generally slow. Their venomous spines provide defense against predators, making them one of the ocean's most dangerous fish. They belong to the family ***Scorpaenidae*** and to the genus ***Scorpaena***.

DID YOU KNOW?

The Scorpionfish can change its color to blend in with the background.

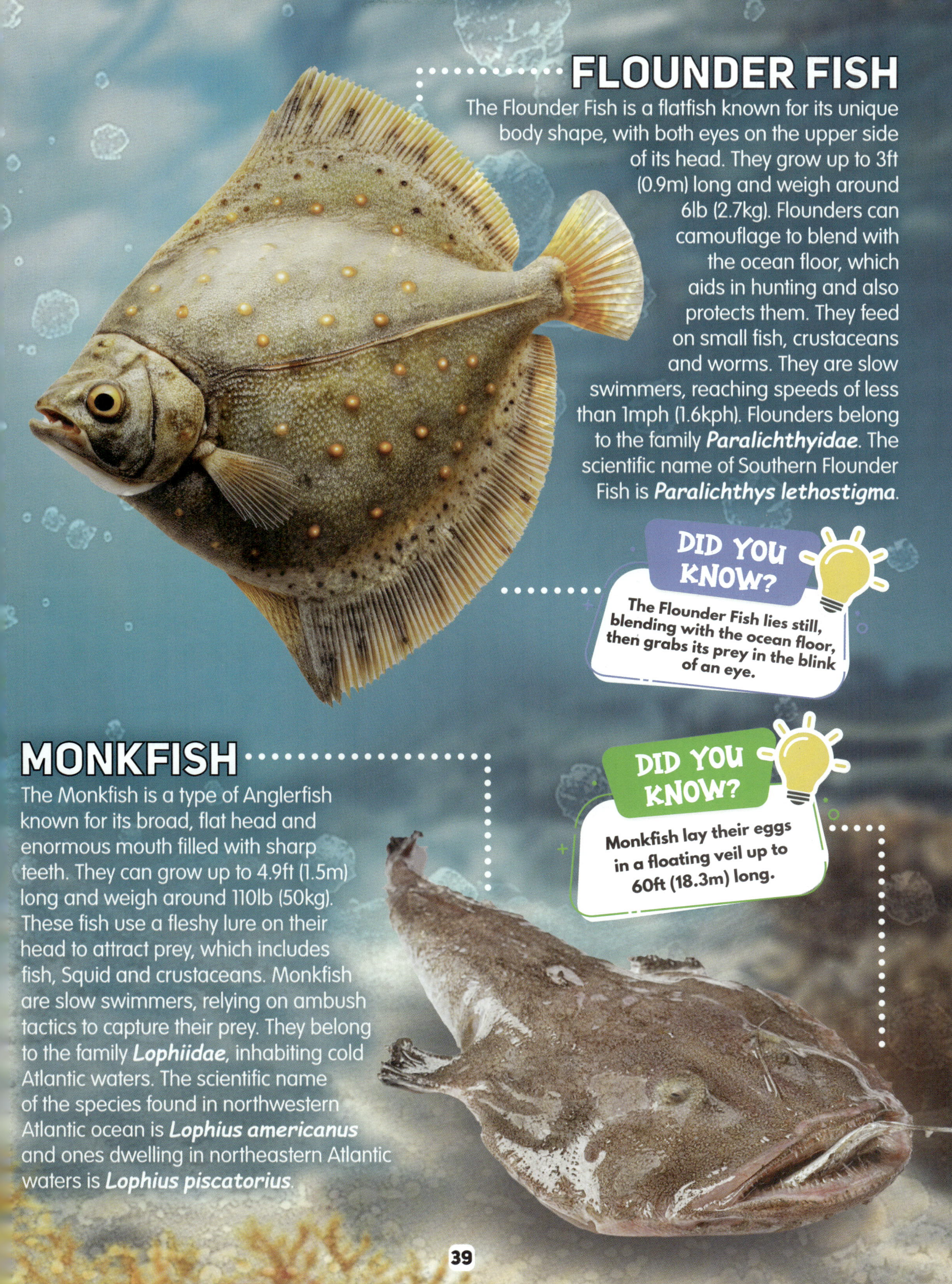

FLOUNDER FISH

The Flounder Fish is a flatfish known for its unique body shape, with both eyes on the upper side of its head. They grow up to 3ft (0.9m) long and weigh around 6lb (2.7kg). Flounders can camouflage to blend with the ocean floor, which aids in hunting and also protects them. They feed on small fish, crustaceans and worms. They are slow swimmers, reaching speeds of less than 1mph (1.6kph). Flounders belong to the family ***Paralichthyidae***. The scientific name of Southern Flounder Fish is ***Paralichthys lethostigma***.

DID YOU KNOW?

The Flounder Fish lies still, blending with the ocean floor, then grabs its prey in the blink of an eye.

MONKFISH

The Monkfish is a type of Anglerfish known for its broad, flat head and enormous mouth filled with sharp teeth. They can grow up to 4.9ft (1.5m) long and weigh around 110lb (50kg). These fish use a fleshy lure on their head to attract prey, which includes fish, Squid and crustaceans. Monkfish are slow swimmers, relying on ambush tactics to capture their prey. They belong to the family ***Lophiidae***, inhabiting cold Atlantic waters. The scientific name of the species found in northwestern Atlantic ocean is ***Lophius americanus*** and ones dwelling in northeastern Atlantic waters is ***Lophius piscatorius***.

DID YOU KNOW?

Monkfish lay their eggs in a floating veil up to 60ft (18.3m) long.

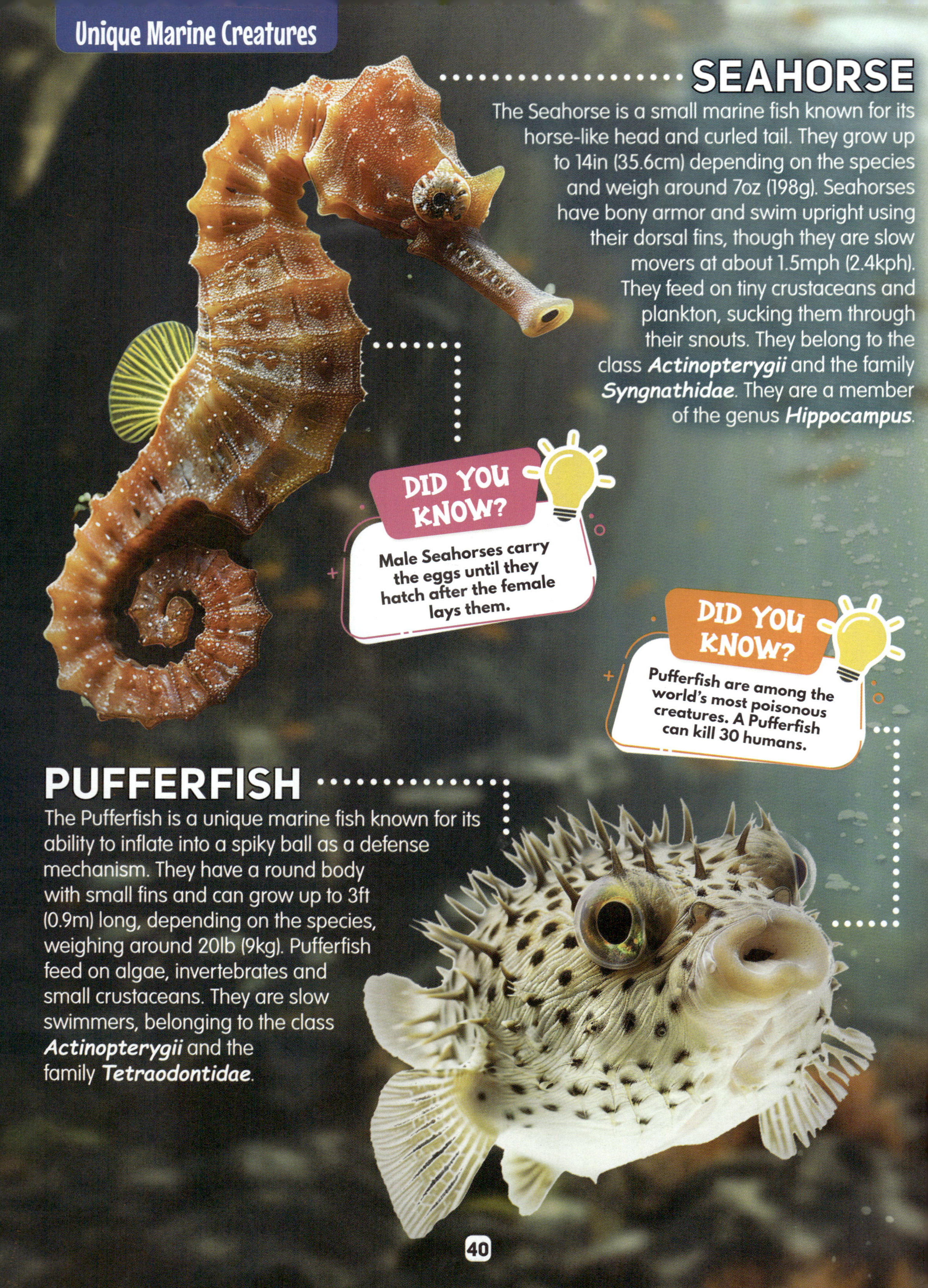

SEAHORSE

The Seahorse is a small marine fish known for its horse-like head and curled tail. They grow up to 14in (35.6cm) depending on the species and weigh around 7oz (198g). Seahorses have bony armor and swim upright using their dorsal fins, though they are slow movers at about 1.5mph (2.4kph). They feed on tiny crustaceans and plankton, sucking them through their snouts. They belong to the class ***Actinopterygii*** and the family ***Syngnathidae***. They are a member of the genus ***Hippocampus***.

PUFFERFISH

The Pufferfish is a unique marine fish known for its ability to inflate into a spiky ball as a defense mechanism. They have a round body with small fins and can grow up to 3ft (0.9m) long, depending on the species, weighing around 20lb (9kg). Pufferfish feed on algae, invertebrates and small crustaceans. They are slow swimmers, belonging to the class ***Actinopterygii*** and the family ***Tetraodontidae***.

JELLYFISH

The Jellyfish is a fascinating marine animal with a soft, umbrella-shaped body and trailing tentacles. Their bodies are 95 percent water, making them lightweight, with masses varying from a few ounces to over 200lb (91kg) in larger species like the Lion's Mane Jellyfish. Sizes range from less than an inch to 6.5ft (2m) in diameter. They move passively with currents, but can pulse their bell to swim at speeds up to 5mph (8kph). Jellyfish feed on plankton, small fish and crustaceans, using their tentacles' stinging cells. They belong to the class ***Scyphozoa***. Their scientific name varies with the species.

DID YOU KNOW?

Jellyfish don't have brains, hearts or bones.

LEAFY SEADRAGON

The Leafy Seadragon is a fascinating marine fish known for its leafy appendages, which help it blend with seaweed and kelp. It grows up to 1.5ft (0.4m) long and weighs about 0.5lb (0.23kg). The Seadragons feed on small crustaceans and plankton. They are slow swimmers, relying on their camouflage for protection. They are native to the waters of southern and western Australia. Leafy Seadragons belong to the family ***Syngnathidae***. Their scientific name is ***Phycodurus eques***.

DID YOU KNOW?

A Leafy Seadragon has fins on its head for turning or steering and a dorsal fin to propel itself.

CUTTLEFISH

The Cuttlefish is a highly intelligent cephalopod known for its ability to change color and texture. They have a soft, bulbous body with a fin running along each side and a unique internal shell called the cuttlebone. Cuttlefish grow up to 24in (61cm) long and weigh around 7–23lb (3–10.4kg). They are fast swimmers, capable of reaching speeds of 25mph (40kph). Cuttlefish feed on small fish and crustaceans. They belong to the class ***Cephalopoda*** and family ***Sepiidae***. Their scientific name is ***Sepia officinalis***.

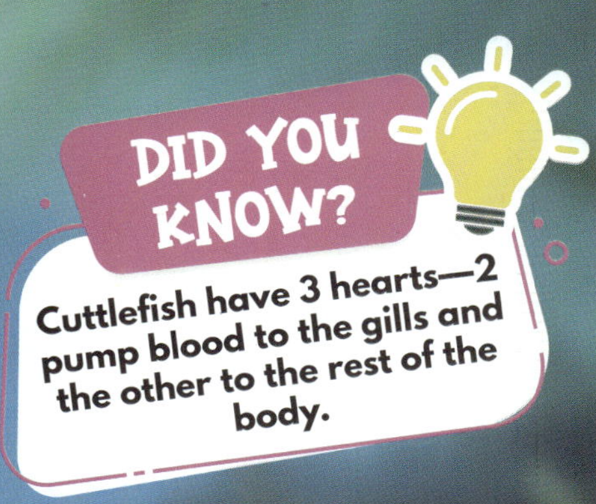

STARFISH

The Starfish or Sea Star is a marine invertebrate known for its star-shaped body, typically having 5 arms. It can grow up to 12in (30.5cm) across, with a mass of around 11lb (5kg). Starfish move slowly using tube feet, reaching speeds of about 10ydph* (0.01kph). They feed on mollusks, such as Clams and Oysters, using their stomach to digest food outside their bodies. They belong to the class ***Asteroidea*** and the family ***Asteriidae***.

DID YOU KNOW?

Starfish can regenerate a lost limb or even an entire body from a severed body part.

* ydph: yards per hour

GIANT OCEANIC MANTA RAY

The Giant Oceanic Manta Ray is the largest ray species, reaching up to 23ft (7m) across and weighing around 3,000lb (1,360kg). With triangular pectoral fins and a long tail, it glides gracefully through the ocean at speeds of up to 20mph (32kph). This gentle filter feeder consumes plankton and small fish by swimming with its mouth open. It belongs to the family ***Mobulidae***, inhabiting tropical and subtropical waters. Its scientific name is ***Manta birostris***.

DID YOU KNOW?

It has a high brain-to-body weight ratio, which means its brain is much larger compared to its overall body.

HUMPHEAD WRASSE

The Humphead Wrasse, also known as the Napoleon Wrasse, is one of the largest reef fish, reaching up to 7ft (2.1m) in length and weighing over 400lb (181kg). It has a prominent hump on its forehead, thick lips and vibrant blue-green coloration. This slow swimmer feeds on mollusks, crustaceans and even toxic animals like Crown-Of-Thorns Starfish. It belongs to family ***Labridae***, thriving in Indo-Pacific coral reefs. Its scientific name is ***Cheilinus undulatus***.

DID YOU KNOW?

Humphead Wrasses can change their sex, starting as females and transforming into males later.

OCEAN SUNFISH

The Ocean Sunfish is one of the heaviest bony fish, weighing up to 5,000lb (2,268kg) and reaching lengths of 10ft (3m). They have a flattened, oval-shaped body with long dorsal and anal fins, giving them a unique silhouette. Ocean Sunfish are slow swimmers, moving at about 2mph (3.2kph). As large filter feeders, they consume Jellyfish, small fish, plankton and algae. Found in temperate and tropical oceans, they often bask near the surface, earning the nickname "sunfish." They belong to family ***Molidae*** and their scientific name is ***Mola mola***.

KOI FISH

The Koi Fish, a variety of ornamental Carp, is renowned for its shimmering, metallic scales, giving it a golden appearance. These freshwater fish are admired for their striking patterns and colors. They can grow up to 3ft (0.9m) long and weigh around 35lb (16kg). Kinrin Koi are omnivorous, feeding on algae, insects and plant matter. Though slow swimmers, averaging about 2mph (3.2kph), their graceful movements add to their charm. Native to East Asia, they are a symbol of prosperity and longevity in many cultures. They belong to the family ***Cyprinidae***.

DID YOU KNOW?

Kinrin Koi can thrive in both outdoor ponds and indoor tanks.

DISCUS FISH

The Discus Fish is a vibrant freshwater fish known for its round, disk-shaped body and striking patterns. They typically grow to about 6–8in (15–20cm) long and weigh up to 8.8oz (250g). Found in the Amazon River Basin, they prefer warm, slow-moving waters. Discus Fish feed on algae, small invertebrates and plant matter. Though not fast swimmers, their graceful movements add to their appeal in aquariums. They belong to the family ***Cichlidae*** and their scientific name is ***Symphysodon***.

DID YOU KNOW?

It can change its color to a certain extent depending on the environment and personal factors.

FLOWERHORN CICHLID

The Flowerhorn Cichlid is a vibrant freshwater fish known for the distinctive hump on its head and bold, colorful patterns. They typically grow up to 16in (41cm) long and weigh around 2.2lb (1kg). Flowerhorns are omnivores, feeding on pellets, small fish and plant matter. While they are not fast swimmers, they are agile and active. Belonging to the family ***Cichlidae***, Flowerhorns are popular aquarium fish due to their striking appearance and unique charm.

DID YOU KNOW?

In many cultures, Flowerhorns are believed to bring good luck and prosperity.

SEA TURTLE

A Sea Turtle is a marine reptile known for its hard, protective shells. They can grow up to 6.5ft (2m) in length and weigh over 1,000lb (454kg). These Turtles, besides their slow-moving disposition can reach speeds of up to 22mph (35kph) when threatened. They primarily feed on Jellyfish, seaweed and small marine animals. Sea Turtles belong to the families, ***Cheloniidae*** (Flatback Sea Turtle, Green Turtles and others) and ***Dermochalyidae*** (Leatherback Turtles). The scientific name of the Green Sea Turtle is ***Chelonia mydas*** and the Leatherback Sea Turtle is ***Dermochelys coriacea***.

SALTWATER CROCODILE

The Saltwater Crocodile is the largest living reptile, reaching up to 23ft (7m) and weighing over 2,200lb (998kg). Known for its powerful jaws, it primarily feeds on fish, birds and mammals. As a marine reptile, it is an excellent swimmer and can reach speeds of 18mph (29kph) in short bursts. Found in coastal regions of Southeast Asia and northern Australia, it belongs to the family ***Crocodylidae***. Its scientific name is ***Crocodylus porosus***.